FIFTY
FASHION
LOOKS
THAT
CHANGED
THE
1990s

DESIGN
MUSEUM

FIFTY
FASHION
LOOKS

THAT
CHANGED
THE
1990s

**PAULA
REED**

 conran
OCTOPUS

THE
1990s

Above: sleek and sexy minimalism was the leitmotif of the 1990s. Dress by Azzedine Alaïa. Previous page: Supermodel Linda Evangelista wears a black-and-white ready-to-wear evening gown with a matching jacket by designer Valentino Garavani for his Italian fashion house Valentino at the Spring-Summer 1992 fashion show in Paris.

Above: Kate Moss (second from right) was, arguably, the face of the 1990s. Below: The model Veronica Webb walks down the catwalk in Donna Karan's Autumn 1994 show.

THE
1990s

The financial boom and flamboyance of the 1980s ceded to a decade of soul searching. A new generation of designers kicked against the accepted confines of high fashion and dedicated themselves to defining modernity. Political and cultural upheaval, economic crisis, famine in Africa and the fear visited by the Chernobyl disaster, provided a backdrop for a fashion style that was dark and conceptual.

The Paris catwalks embraced the diversity of both traditional couturiers and the avant-garde whose standard-bearers were the 'Antwerp Six' (see page 96). For the first half of the decade it looked as if anti-fashion would make the most lasting mark on the industry at the end of the century. The UK provided a much-needed injection of energy, flair and showmanship, as the Alexander McQueen was installed at Givenchy and John Galliano at Christian Dior.

The technological revolution blurred boundaries and divisions. Designers now planned their collections for maximum video impact and the international fashion shows become theatrical spectacles that only partly reflected the clothes for sale in the shops. Fashion writers crouched over word processors instead of typewriters. Pattern cutters worked on computer instead of card. Art directors laid out their pages using desktop publishing software.

Fashion was no longer a coterie of family businesses but a network of vast international conglomerates. In a world that had elevated the pursuit of luxury and at the same time demoted 'gowns' to 'frocks' and 'dedicated followers' to 'fashion victims', nothing would ever be the same again.

The Danish supermodel Helena Christensen backstage before a 1994 Autumn/Winter catwalk show. The early 1990s saw the second great flourishing of catwalk supermodels who became celebrities in their own right.

AIR JORDANS

Sneakers get serious

The 1990s were sneaker obsessed, as a growing number of sports shoes became the focus of a massive fashion cult. Trainers were endorsed by celebrities and sports stars alike, but the daddy of them all was the basketball player Michael Jordan (1963–).

Michael Jordan was famous for his ability to 'catch air', jumping higher than seemed humanly possible. But, in terms of money alone, his earnings as a fashion face would eclipse his most spectacular achievements on the basketball court. In 1985 'His Airness' became the crown prince of athletic shoe endorsements, with the launch of Nike's Air Jordan line. The shoe he helped design would go on to have a history almost as illustrious as that of the man himself. By 1998 Jordan had reportedly made over $130 million from Nike alone.

The line was backed by a savvy marketing campaign, featuring 'MJ' himself. One of Jordan's more popular commercials for the shoe involved film director Spike Lee reprising the role of Mars Blackmon, a character from Lee's own *She's Gotta Have It* (1986), who is a fanatical supporter of the New York Knicks. In the commercials, Blackmon desperately seeks to track down the secret behind Jordan's abilities and becomes convinced that 'It's gotta be the shoes.' Such was the hype surrounding the sneakers that there was even a spate of 'shoe-jackings', in which people were robbed of their Jordans at gunpoint.

The AJ1 model. Ironically, the black detailing on Air Jordans made them 'illegal' on the basketball court, according to National Basketball Association rules. That didn't, however, stop Michael Jordan from repeatedly wearing them.

JULIA ROBERTS IN
PRETTY WOMAN
The decade's celluloid sweetheart

The wardrobe for *Pretty Woman*, the 1990 film that marked the turning point in the career of the then 23-year-old Julia Roberts (1967–), still looks remarkably chic. The polka-dotted brown dress (with matching hat) that Julia, as Vivian, chose for the polo match, the red gown she wore to the opera, and even the midriff-baring hooker dress are all silhouettes that could still easily be worn, decades after the movie's release.

But, aside from achieving fashion credentials, the costumes had a more subtle function. Every detail had to reflect the evolution of Vivian's character: her rags-to-riches transition from tart with a heart to trophy wife for the Richard Gere character, Edward. As the movie's costume designer, Marilyn Vance, explained, 'In the beginning, she's wearing so much "stuff": a jacket, those boots, the hat, it's all very busy. In each successive look, you begin to see her take his "less is more" direction. By the end, she's very simply put together – pure sophistication.'

Aside from a pair of Chanel heels and the tie that Vivian wears (with nothing else) to greet Edward when he returns to the hotel after work, the costume department created all of the iconic fashion moments in the Oscar-nominated film. The midriff-baring dress, for instance, was inspired by a vintage 1960s bathing suit that Vance herself owned.

If the studio bosses had got their way, the famous red dress would have been black. 'But I knew it needed to be red,' Vance said. 'Before the decision was made, we ended up having to create three different dresses. We took every colour, lit it and shot her. […]Finally, I was able to find the right shade and convince everyone to go in my direction.'

Right: From hooker to trophy wife – Julia Robert's clothes in *Pretty Woman* mirror her Eliza Doolittle-like transformation
Below: The famous polka-dotted brown dress.

LADY MISS KIER

Deee-Lite reignites disco

Deee-Lite, and its lead singer Lady Miss Kier, shot to stardom in 1990 with the smash hit 'Groove is in the Heart'. She was born Kierin Magenta Kirby (1963–) in a small town in Ohio. She moved to New York to study fashion design and saw a ready-made market for her disco-ready clothing among friends whom she met on the club scene – Disney-princess-pink for the girls and blue glitter suits for the boys, all set off to perfection by silver platform boots.

The Deee-Lite team: for a few, dizzying, 1990s moments, some experts rated Lady Miss Kier as serious competition for Madonna herself.

One of her clients was the Russian DJ Dmitry Brill, who persuaded her to record a demo with him and the Japanese DJ Towa Tei. The result was the disco–house–funk fusion that was Deee-Lite, in which Kirby's gorgeously soulful voice was backed up by a funky, highly danceable beat. It was the music that came to define the early '90s club culture of New York City.

It was Kirby who created the exuberant look of the band, forging for herself the fantasy alter ego of Lady Miss Kier, the ultimate club diva. With her white-powdered face, razor-sharp drawn-on brows and 7.6-cm (3-in) fake eyelashes, Lady Miss Kier was like a female drag queen. She took the colourful 1960s retro influences that were circling the club and street scene at the time and nailed them to the Deee-Lite fashion wall, creating a stage-worthy look that involved Pucci cat suits, candy-coloured minidresses, towering platforms, sculptural heels and a gravity-defying flicked-up hairdo.

STEVEN MEISEL

1990

The supermodels' Svengali

In the war between publishing giants Condé Nast and Hearst, photographers were the magazines' most potent weapons. Steven Meisel (1954–), signed exclusively to *Vogue*, ended up being the highest-paid photographer of the time. His very controlled, unashamedly artificial and often provocative style defined the look not only of fashion magazine spreads, but also of many of the big fashion campaigns of the decade – from Dolce & Gabbana to Valentino, Calvin Klein and Gap. And his was the lens that captured Madonna at her most unencumbered in her notorious book *Sex* (1992).

    With his poker-straight black hair, unlined olive skin, arching dark brows and inscrutable black eyes, Meisel cut an exotic figure, even in an industry where the unusual is normal. In spite of only ever wearing black, he could easily be spotted across a dark runway in his 'uniform' of trench coat and flap-eared, rabbit-fur hat (winter) or black bucket hat (summer).

    Linda Evangelista was his muse. He worked with her more than any of the other supermodels. His photographs of Christy Turlington, Naomi Campbell and Evangelista defined their iconic status. It was Meisel who packaged them as 'The Trinity', transforming them from individual superstars into a collective fashion force. Cindy Crawford once tried to explain his Midas touch: 'He makes you believe in what it is you are supposed to be the minute you walk in the door. You walk out thinking you took the most brilliant pictures ever.'

Steven Meisel out clubbing with Naomi Campbell in 1990. Despite his starry friends, Meisel is notoriously reticent with the media and dislikes being photographed.

KATE MOSS / CORINNE DAY   1990
Fashioning the world's most influential waif

Kate Moss's remarkable career was launched in the July 1990 issue of *The Face*. The photographer who was instrumental in her success was Corinne Day (1962–2010), who, with stylist Melanie Ward, shot the 16-year-old model on England's Camber Sands for the eight-page editorial 'The Third Summer of Love'.

Corinne Day had learned how to use a camera while she was working as a model in Milan. Her simple, documentary style was a reaction against what she saw as the remoteness of high fashion. She hated the models of the time, dismissing their look as 'stale, just about sex and glamour, when there are other elements of beauty'. The scraggy-haired Croydon schoolgirl Kate Moss (1974–), a rank beginner at the model agency Storm, instantly appealed to her. Together, they revolutionized fashion photography.

Model and photographer were commissioned for a cover shoot for the March 1993 issue of British *Vogue*, and Moss's transition from the niche style press to the mainstream was complete. The image of the doe-eyed Moss, staring out of that cover, her hair scraped back and face unadorned, presented the fashion industry with a seductive alternative to the Amazonian 'Big Six' supermodels.

The potent combination of Kate Moss and Corinne Day turned fashion on its head and kicked off the whole grunge movement in the 1990s in a blaze of controversy. The bemused debate over how Moss could ever have become a model – at her height, with no boobs, bandy legs and such knobbly knees – would rumble on for years.

Kate Moss's fresh-faced looks and Corinne Day's unencumbered photographic style were first brought together in the July 1990 'Third Summer of Love' issue of *The Face*. Their relationship was cemented in 1993 when Corinne photographed Moss for the front cover of British *Vogue*.

GANGSTA RAP

The sound of the mean streets

In the 1990s hip-hop ceded to gangsta rap. By the middle of the decade, the key influence in hip-hop fashion came from the dress styles of street thugs and prison inmates. Gangsta rappers such as N W A (Niggaz Wit Attitude), Wu-Tang Clan and Gang Starr wore Chuckie's khaki pants, plaid shirts and white Champion T-shirts, Raiders Starter jackets and a plethora of logos. They accessorized with Carhartt and Timberland, Chuck Taylor sneakers, black Raiders baseball caps, and bandannas.

The style of wearing trousers saggy and low-slung, without a belt, emulated the look of offenders whose belts and shoelaces were removed when they arrived in prison.

Of the mainstream fashion brands, Tommy Hilfiger (see pages 80–1) was anointed the rappers' brand of choice after Snoop Dogg wore a Hilfiger sweatshirt during an appearance on *Saturday Night Live*. Hilfiger's perceived waspy exclusivity made it desirable, and New York stores sold out of the Snoop Dogg shirts within 24 hours of the show. Hilfiger courted the new market, featuring black models in the company's advertising campaigns, and rappers like Puffy and Coolio on his runways.

Hip-hop fashion became big business as white kids in the suburbs developed a taste for the streetwise wardrobe. Brands like Phat Farm, Sean John and Rocawear made hundreds of millions of dollars dealing in mainstream hip-hop fashion.

Ice Cube, one of the founders of gangsta rap, in 1991. Gangsta's political and violent lyrics were matched by a look that was at once aggressive and aspirational.

'HAMMER PANTS'

'You can move in 'em. You can dance in 'em'

In the beginning they were called 'parachute pants'. This, undoubtedly, had something to do with the way the fabric ballooned around the crotch and thigh whenever the wearer moved. But, in the 1000c, B-boye and B-girls (better known by their media misnomer 'breakdancers') loved them. The loose fit allowed them to move with ease. They were particularly useful if cut in nylon or some comparably slippery synthetic – all the better to spin or slide in.

Along with a nylon tracksuit, parachute pants were standard issue for any self-respecting B-boy at the time. As described by author Vicky Carnegy, 'serious dancing meant a serious dance style – clothes that were eye-catching but also comfortable to move in'. The athletic and often extremely dangerous dance moves caught the attention of the mainstream in a number of films (*Wild Style*, *Breakin'* and *Delivery Boys* among them) and, consequently, their fashion influence spread.

Then, in 1990, along came Stanley Burrell (1962–), the artist known as MC Hammer, who inspired the term 'Hammer pants' after he appeared in a customized pair of parachute pants in the video for his hit 'U Can't Touch This'. Hammer's version was tight at the ankle and extremely baggy at the crotch, making them perfect for his on-stage antics.

Burrell neatly summed up the appeal of the pants that ever after were known by his name: 'You can make a fashion statement,' he said. 'You can move in 'em. You can dance in 'em. [...] It accentuates the movement, and it gives you freedom of movement. [...] You move, and then the pants move, so it brings a nice little flair.'

MC Hammer's flamboyant stage outfits invariably included 'Hammer pants' – loose-fitting trousers, somewhere between Turkish harem trousers and the Indian dhoti.

SUPERMODELS
Bankable beauties

Naomi Campbell, Linda Evangelista, Tatjana Patitz, Christy Turlington and Cindy Crawford officially crossed over into uncharted territory of modelling fame in January 1990, when they appeared on the cover of British *Vogue*, shot by Peter Lindbergh. This was undoubtedly the moment when these fabled beauties, all of them wrapped in Giorgio di Sant' Angelo jersey and all of them established household names, were raised to the pantheon of 'supermodels'.

Along with Claudia Schiffer, they were termed the 'Big Six' and quickly established credentials well beyond the confines of fashion. They appeared on talk shows, dominated daily gossip columns, landed movie roles, dated or married film stars, and earned fortunes. Fame empowered them to market themselves as global brands commanding higher and higher fees. Christy Turlington's contract with Maybelline earned her $800,000 for just 12 days' work each year. In 1995 Claudia Schiffer reportedly racked up a startling $12 million for her year's work.

The supermodel phenomenon, however, scarcely outlasted the decade. By the late 1990s pop singers and actresses were already beginning to oust professional models from the covers of fashion magazines. Celebrity rather than outright beauty moved into the limelight. Schiffer theorized: 'In order to become a supermodel one must be on all the covers all over the world at the same time so that people can recognize the girls. That is, for now, not possible, not least because the advertising industry is very much taken nowadays by pop stars and actresses. Supermodels like we once were don't exist any more.'

Supermodels in the ascendance. Linda Evangelista, Cindy Crawford, Naomi Campbell and Christy Turlington on the Versace catwalk in 1991.

22

PATRICK DEMARCHELIER PHOTOGRAPHS DIANA, PRINCESS OF WALES

1991

A new decade, a new Diana

In the 1990s the Princess of Wales's 'lamb dressed as mutton' wardrobe was gradually replaced with one of simple sophistication. She had worked out what suited her best and now favoured a style that was elegantly pared down and flattered a honed and fit body. After years of being celebrated as a fashion icon she actually became one. The pictures that, arguably, changed everything were commissioned in 1991 by British *Vogue* editor Liz Tilberis, for a cover of the magazine. They were styled by Diana's trusted wardrobe advisor, the magazine's deputy editor Anna Harvey. The photographer was the Frenchman Patrick Demarchelier (1943–).

Royal observers often labelled Demarchelier's photographs of Princess Diana as 'iconoclastic'. No one, it seemed, had ever imagined a royal portrait could look like that. Diana appointed Demarchelier her personal portraitist, which made him the first non-Briton to fill such a role for the Royal Family. He was to photograph her many times for British *Vogue* and, later, when Liz Tilberis moved to New York, for *Harper's Bazaar*. It was for *Bazaar* that he produced the well-known black-and-white photo of the Princess wearing a strapless dress, a tiara and a luminous smile. His pictures were borderline shocking at the time because of their informality and spontaneity.

Demarchelier astutely identified key things about the princess that no other photographer had managed to capture. 'Diana was funny and kind but fundamentally she was a very simple woman who liked very simple things,' he said. 'She looked both in control and sweetly vulnerable, with plenty of her typical coyness.'

Patrick Demarchelier at a photoshoot (above) and in his studio (below) where his famous photograph of Diana for the December 1991 cover of *Vogue* can be seen.

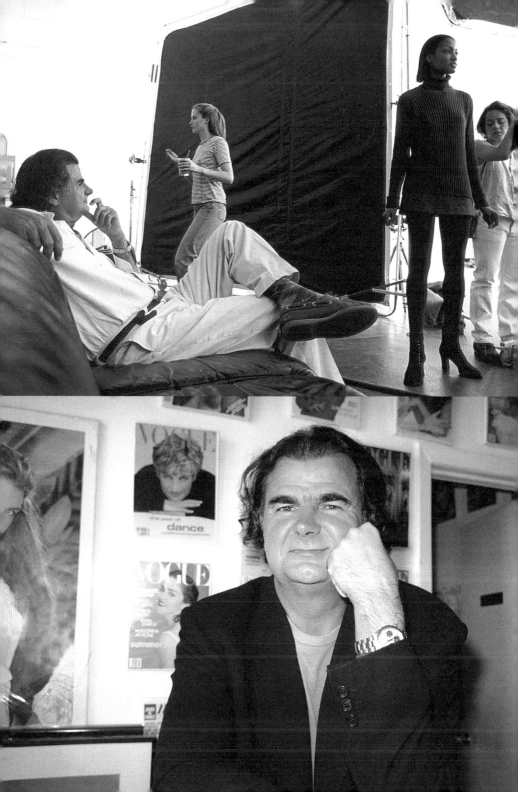

ABSOLUTELY FABULOUS

Sending up the fashionistas

Edina (Eddy) Monsoon and Eurydice Colette Clytemnestra Dido Bathsheba Rabelais Patricia Cocteau Stone, known as Patsy Stone, were career women on the London fashion scene. Eddy ran her own PR firm, whose only regular client was the singer Lulu, and the only member of staff an assistant called Bubble. Patsy was a well-paid fashion editor without portfolio on a glossy magazine, with an exaggerated sense of her own importance: 'One snap of my fingers and I can raise hemlines so high, the world is your gynaecologist.'

Edina was mildly overweight, a fact she tried to disguise with flamboyant layers of the latest designer must-haves. Patsy was comparatively stylishly dressed, often in something Chanel-esque, and wore her hair in a characteristic blonde beehive. She claimed not to have eaten anything since 1973. Precious little work ever seemed to be done, but the boozy besties could certainly put an eye-catching look together, spending their nights fuelled by a combination of 'Stoli' and 'Bolli', and many of their daylight hours engaged in marathon shopping sprees at 'Harvey Nicks'.

Despite its merciless and hilarious send-up of the fashion industry and the cult of celebrity, *Absolutely Fabulous*, first aired in 1992, had no shortage of 'celebs' lining up for guest appearances. Curiously, too, it often managed to hype what it sought to ridicule. *Ab Fab* made designer Christian Lacroix a household name after an episode featured him in a scene shot in his Sloane Street shop.

Patsy and Eddy strut their stuff during an episode of *Absolutely Fabulous*. The duo's ridiculous clothes satirized the gulf between glamorous image and imperfect reality that has always been the 'dark side' of fashion.

CLAUDIA SCHIFFER

Fashion's favourite sex kitten

In 1987 the teenage Claudia Schiffer (1970–) was spotted at a Düsseldorf disco by the owner of a modelling agency. She was aiming to go to law school, but her parents were persuaded to let her go to Paris instead. Schiffer, who at the time felt slightly awkward about her height and looks, was convinced that it would come to nothing: 'After I was discovered, and did the test shots, I was sure that they would realize they had made a mistake and send me back.'

As it turned out, there had been no mistake. Schiffer's springboard to fame came in 1990 in the shape of a Guess jeans campaign, shot by the then relatively unknown photographer Ellen von Unwerth. Von Unwerth created for the model a playfully sexy image that capitalized on her likeness to the kittenish Brigitte Bardot. She rose to the dizzying heights of supermodel stardom as a favourite of Karl Lagerfeld and would eventually appear on the covers of more than 500 magazines, including *Vogue, Cosmopolitan* and the iconic music magazine *Rolling Stone*, becoming the first model ever to do so. She walked virtually every major designer's runway and became nearly omnipresent in marketing campaigns.

Schiffer was the first great supermodel of the 1990s, attracting fees as high as $50,000 a day and earning millions more through licensing and endorsements.

Claudia Schiffer in Paris in 1992. Schiffer's reign as queen of the catwalk in the early 1990s heralded the second great generation of supermodels.

JOE McKENNA
The stylists' stylist

Joe McKenna may not be a household name, but he is the quintessential industry insider: the *éminence grise* behind some of the most influential fashion imagery of the decade. Whether it's for Calvin Klein, Yves Saint Laurent, Versace or Jil Sander, Banana Republic or Gap, the McKenna signature is one of uncompromising simplicity and precision. In the decade when fashion was in thrall to the discipline of minimalism, he became the stylists' stylist.

Born just outside Glasgow, McKenna moved to New York in 1986, initially working at *Vanity Fair* and *Rolling Stone*. In the 1990s he styled Calvin Klein's CK One ads, working with photographer Steven Meisel (see pages 14–15). He also started a long and close association with Azzedine Alaïa and Jil Sander, whose advertising images he styled, setting a new standard for high-fashion glamour. However, his most engaging and enduring projects have arguably been with Bruce Weber. McKenna's discovery of the photographer's sexed-up naturalism was a career-defining epiphany for the boy from Kirkintilloch, and their collaborations yielded some of the most daring images of the time.

In 1992, and again in 1998, McKenna published *Joe's*, a magazine that was a showcase for the photographers he worked with, a soapbox for the designers who employed him and a shop window for ideas unencumbered by the commercial demands of the newsstand. There may only have been two issues but they still change hands on the Internet at prices that are escalating faster than blue-chip stock. At the height of the supermodel era, McKenna gave his first cover over to the Virgin Mary, who was depicted gazing upward and serenely exhaling a ribbon of smoke.

A spread from the first issue of *Joe's* magazine featuring Stuart Friedman. Joe McKenna's high-concept journal helped to secure his position as the 'stylists' stylist'.

LIZ TILBERIS

The lady who rebooted American style

It can be said, without any exaggeration, that Grace Coddington (see pages 72–3), Anna Wintour (see pages 106–7) and Liz Tilberis (1947–99) were the three British women who forever changed fashion in the 1990s. All three had been colleagues at British *Vogue*. Coddington and Wintour went to US *Vogue* in 1988. Tilberis followed them to New York in 1992, to be editor-in-chief of the magazine's main rival – and the United States' first fashion journal *Harper's Bazaar*.

At the time, the magazine was long past its heyday and competition in New York was fierce and relentless. It was feared that Tilberis, known for her warmth and humility, was a lamb to the slaughter. Certainly, it was a lonely time for her, as the industry waited with perfectly plucked eyebrows to see if she would succeed or fail. Her secret weapon, however, was the French art director Fabien Baron. Together, they helped usher in a minimalist aesthetic that perfectly reflected the fashion *zeitgeist* of the 1990s.

Baron's 1992 redesign is still a benchmark in the magazine world. The magazine's new style was characterized by layouts breezy with cool white space, tempered by the use of bold, overlapping typography. Photographs, and their creators, were treated with a new respect.

The style of the revamped magazine took all of *Bazaar*'s competitors by storm, and it was quickly dubbed 'the world's most beautiful fashion magazine'. With the winning combination of Baron's artistic virtuosity and Tilberis's vision of practical, democratic fashion, the duo created a magazine that was a few degrees cooler than its brasher rivals and which took understated glamour as its blueprint.

Liz Tilberis at her desk in 1992, freshly appointed editor-in-chief of *Harper's Bazaar*. Her reinvigoration of the venerable but tired fashion magazine first astounded and then delighted the New York fashion scene.

CALVIN KLEIN

Minimalism and provocation

Hard to credit it, but at the end of the 1980s Calvin Klein (1942–), the genius of the American designer jeans boom, was facing bankruptcy. In the course of the 1990s, he reinvented himself as fashion's master minimalist and made a vast fortune with his underwear, fragrance and secondary CK lines. Fashion was primed and ready for Klein's minimalist aesthetic. After the excesses of the 1980s and troubled by the political upheaval caused by the recession and the war in the Gulf, the establishment embraced the new simplicity. The language of architects started to appear in catwalk press releases.

But Klein's masterstroke was his ability to lace what could easily have remained a high-fashion aesthetic with outright provocation, and thereby spread his message on a mass commercial scale. He had already proved, with his controversial jeans ads featuring the young Brooke Shields in the 1980s, that he was not afraid of ruffling fashion's feathers. In the 1990s, now with the waiflike Kate Moss as the face of his brand, he explored the outer reaches of sex and androgyny. An especially controversial advertising image for Calvin Klein Jeans in 1995 even led to accusations of child pornography.

Klein cemented his high-fashion status in 1993 by being named both the womenswear and menswear designer of the year by the Council of Fashion Designers of America. His advertisements may have been deemed inappropriate, but his design philosophy remained consistent: sexy, clean and minimal.

Herb Ritts's image of the pop singer (and, later, actor) Mark Wahlberg was a typical example of Klein's provocative, in-your-face advertising, at once shocking and titillating.

BENETTON / OLIVIERO TOSCANI 1992
Politically incorrect advertising

In the 1980s Oliviero Toscani (1942–) created an iconic but cosy advertising campaign featuring multiethnic models for the mass-market knitwear retailer Benetton. But in the 1990s the ads became progressively edgy and more controversial. They tackled topics such as race, politics, social issues and sexuality. There were images of a nun kissing a priest, and the bloodied uniform of a Bosnian soldier. One of the most controversial was the picture captured of AIDS activist David Kirby on his deathbed, surrounded by his family.

The image of a nun kissing a priest was a calculated provocation, especially given the fact that Benetton was an Italian company, but its shock value was mild in comparison with what was to follow.

During Toscani's time as art director and photographer for Benetton in the 1990s, the company's advertising never featured a single branded product in their mainstream campaigns. The brand gave Toscani free rein and he relentlessly turned up the heat of public outrage with each new set of photographs. He defined Benetton as a brand in pursuit of the provocative and controversial, one that was never afraid to engage in topical debate.

In spite of product playing second fiddle to the message, sales rose and Benetton became one of the best-known clothing brands in the world. Toscani himself seemed to believe he had a higher calling. 'I am not here to sell pullovers,' he said, 'but to promote an image. […] Benetton's advertising draws public attention to universal themes.' But, eventually, the ads began to cause costly rifts with consumers and retailers. In 1995 Benetton was sued by German retailers, who argued that Toscani's images sabotaged their sales efforts. An image of US prisoners on death row, including their names and the dates of their execution, proved the final straw. The furore that followed was the catalyst for Toscani's departure from the company.

UNITED COLORS
OF BENETTON.

ACID HOUSE
The ecstasy of dance

After Britain's 'Second Summer of Love' in 1988, rave established itself as a massive youth subculture. Its beginnings were innocent enough. As in the hedonistic days of the Summer of Love in San Francisco two decades earlier, the general idea was to 'turn on, tune in and drop out'. Impromptu (and illegal) raves drew revellers in tie-dyed T-shirts, first in their hundreds and then in their thousands. The repetitive, driving dance beats had a psychedelic flavour, and LSD once again became the fashionable drug of choice. It was when acid house became 'acieeeeed' that rave culture, in the eyes of the tabloid press at least, became a threat to the very moral fabric of society. But by then it had also been embraced by many as part of the mainstream.

The rave scene always had its own fashions, but it was not designer-led. The hedonistic DIY aesthetic of acid house was a spontaneous style statement that belonged to rave alone; these revellers needed no help from Paris or New York to get their look together. Acid-bright colours, luminous work jackets and white gloves popped in the strobe lights. Elements of boho chic, tie-dyed T-shirts and beaded jewellery, meanwhile, forged a link with hippy hedonism. Boiler suits, dungarees and Kicker shoes were easy to dance in for hours and hours on end. And the accessories of choice were whistles, glow sticks and adult-sized dummies. The London club Fantazia's smiley face T-shirt was one of the decade's must-haves.

Right and below: The often arcane stylings adopted by acid house revellers might seem puzzling, until you remember that the clinical white and Day-Glo colours were chosen especially to show up under the pulsating strobe lights, almost like a hallucinatory dream.

GAP
The global wardrobe essential

In the 1990s a desire for clothes that were unpretentious and comfortable drew customers to Gap in droves. An apparently magical formula of quality, classic design, affordable prices and a (relatively) cool image ensured that Gap became the fashion destination for millions.

Gap (as in 'generation gap') was founded in 1969 by a property developer, Donald Fisher, who opened his first store in San Francisco. It quickly grew into a juggernaut that encompassed clothing, shoes, accessories, fragrances and underwear. Not only did it serve customers' need for these items, it created them. 'Fashion ground to a halt in the 1990s and Gap was there to address the dress-down trend in a big way,' commented one pundit. 'Every six weeks Gap has a fresh assortment – not necessarily new designs but new colours. The customer gets the message straight away.'

Gap didn't just put paid to the idea that fashion was the reserve of the rich. It went further: it made designer labels start to look like a rip-off. Increasingly, it became a badge of honour to bag a bargain, even among the affluent. Marketing analysts termed the trend towards functional clothes the 'commoditization' of fashion. Some critics felt that the designer fashion industry had driven a nail into its own coffin by embracing 'classics', 'simple chic' and 'minimalism' as the key catwalk trends of the decade.

Not even the red carpet, that last bastion of glamour and couture, was beyond the reach of fashion democratization. When Sharon Stone, one of the biggest movie stars of the decade, pitched up on stage at the 1995 Academy Awards wearing a $22 Gap turtleneck teamed with a long black skirt, she sparked a frenzy among shoppers, who drove sales of 'the Sharon Stone shirt' into millions in the months that followed.

The creative collective Art Club 2000 used Gap as the first subject of its performance pieces about brands and their iconography. The images were later reproduced in *The Face* and *Dazed & Confused*.

DOLCE & GABBANA

Milan's rising stars

Domenico Dolce (1958–) grew up near Palermo in Sicily. His partner, Stefano Gabbana (1962–), is from Milan, the heart of the industrial north. As Dolce & Gabbana, the designers have always reflected the extremities of the Italian peninsula: the glossy style of the north and the sensuality of the south. Their catwalks are populated by every manifestation of the archetypal Italian woman: from the Madonna to the whore, from the diva to the debutante. Italian wives, mothers and lovers are the DNA of every Dolce & Gabbana collection.

The pair launched their label in 1985 but it wasn't until the 1990s that they started to achieve international status. The Italian fashion industry is dominated by long-established houses, businesses that operate on a massive industrial scale. It is difficult for a newcomer to break into that exclusive group and almost unheard of for minnows to measure up to the commercial giants. But, by the end of the 1990s, it was reported that Dolce & Gabbana sales had reached around $500 million per year.

The duo built their empire by making women look fantastically sexy. There is nothing ground-breaking about their silhouette or construction. On the contrary, many of their shapes are classics from the pre-feminist era reinterpreted for a contemporary audience. But the designers' keen appreciation of sex appeal and old-fashioned femininity struck a chord with many women, who fell for the promise that, in Dolce & Gabbana, everyone could look like a screen goddess.

Madonna wears Dolce & Gabbana at Wembley Stadium, London, in September 1993, at the opening performance of her 'Girlie' world tour. In the Italian arriviste brand, the 'queen of pop' found the perfect match for her (latest) persona – glamorous, playful and outrageously sexy.

GRUNGE

The triumph of 'unfashion'

Grunge was never meant to be fashionable. In fact, it was so far removed from fashion that it wasn't even anti-fashion. Or, as James Truman, then editor of *Details* magazine, said in 1992, 'It's unfashion.' The fleece layers, flannel shirts, beanie hats and work boots were the everyday wardrobe of the Seattle working class and were adopted by the musicians and acolytes of the underground scene that grew up in the town. In the early 1990s one critic named Seattle 'the worst-dressed town with the best music scene in the world'.

Inasmuch as grunge became street fashion, it was about 'disappearing' as opposed to 'appearing'. It was a way of bowing out of the pressure to conform, a way of saying no to having to look good. The US media and popular culture had long been dominated by images of the body beautiful, and grunge was a look that united people who were striving to have a 'non-look'. Grunge clothes came from flea markets and charity shops and refuse bins, not from the rails of chichi boutiques.

Then, in 1992, Marc Jacobs (see pages 46– 7), designing for Perry Ellis, introduced his now-notorious Spring/Summer 1993 grunge-inspired collection, and turned a no-nonsense style of dressing into a catwalk statement. Jacobs certainly nailed the look: shapeless floral dresses were worn with flannel lumberjack shirts and combat boots by models with scrubbed-clean faces decorated only with nose rings.

This co-option of grunge by the establishment lasted barely a season. In 1994 Kurt Cobain – its poster boy – committed suicide, and the global recession lifted. Thrift shopping became passé and grunge was relegated to a phase that fashion preferred to forget.

American rock band Nirvana was the quintessence of the grunge sound and look. Kurt Cobain, its lead singer, and Courtney Love in 1993.

MARC JACOBS

New York's new star

A graduate of Parsons The New School for Design, Marc Jacobs (1963–) was only 25 when he joined the all-American sportswear house Perry Ellis. It was a risky but not a baseless choice. The young Jacobs managed to reinvest the label with some of its founder's energy, infusing it with a dose of Manhattan street-smart wit. Winners included a red-and-white tablecloth cotton shirt complete with embroidered black ants, and the 'Freudian slip', a shift dress printed with the brooding face of the Austrian psychoanalyst.

Things took a turn for the interesting in October 1992 when he presented his now-legendary 'grunge' collection. It was inspired by the cult that had built up around musicians in Seattle, a city Jacobs admitted he had never visited. It featured floral slip dresses, accessorized with combat boots and knitted beanie hats, and silk shirts printed to look like flannel. Although the collection never made it into the shops, and got Marc Jacobs fired from his first big job, it established him as a singular creative force on New York's Seventh Avenue.

In 1997 came another surprising career choice, when he accepted an appointment as creative director of the 146-year-old French luggage and handbag company Louis Vuitton, whose owner, Bernard Arnault, believed that a fashion collection could put some sizzle into the brand. Jacobs's look for Louis Vuitton began discreetly enough, with LV logos hidden in out-of-the-way places, beneath buttons or on the soles of shoes, but bolder moves were not far behind. He embossed primary-coloured patent leather bags with the logo and he made raincoats scattered with tiny LVs. The critical kudos his collections garnered was matched by an astounding commercial success, with a quadrupling of sales by the middle of the following decade.

Marc Jacobs and actress Tatum O'Neal arrive at the Fashion Designers Awards in New York in 1993. 'Talents like Mr Jacobs have become exceptional,' wrote Amy Spindler of the *New York Times*. 'He has become the most consistently strong, individualistic, real, live, kicking designer in New York.'

MARIO & DAVIDE SORRENTI

Shooting heroin chic

It is the photographer Mario Sorrenti (1971–) who is often credited with creating the controversial look that became known as 'heroin chic'. As the 1980s drew to a close, Sorrenti was introduced to Calvin Klein by Phil Bicker, the art director with whom he worked at *The Face*. In 1993 Klein commissioned him to shoot the advertising campaign for his new fragrance Obsession, and the images that Sorrenti shot of Kate Moss – his girlfriend at the time – launched him into the big league. The campaign proved highly contentious, with both Sorrenti and Moss subjected to a torrent of criticism for taking Twiggy's 'waif' look to another, more sinister, level.

Mario Sorrenti's downbeat approach had much in common with that of his younger brother, Davide (1976–97), also a fashion photographer, whose naturalistic documentary style was so startlingly opposed to the heavily airbrushed, unfeasibly glamorous images of the 1980s. Like his brother, Davide, too, faced accusations that the distracted, blank gaze of his models glamorized heroin addiction. One of Davide's best-known photos showed his painfully thin teenage girlfriend Jaime King lying on a bed, her clothes torn and surrounded by photos of celebrity drug victims including Kurt Cobain. Davide died in 1997, at the age of 20, of causes that were probably related to heroin abuse.

The debate about the responsibilities of the fashion industry would rage on into the next decade. But, meanwhile, fashion's fascination with the natural, unvarnished look that once had been so radical gained acceptance through the work of photographers such as Juergen Teller, Craig McDean and David Sims. Having started as an underground trend, the approach soon went mainstream as more commercial photographers started copying the style.

Mario Sorrenti's naturalistic, downbeat style, evident in this advertising image for Calvin Klein's Obsession, featuring the young Kate Moss, heralded a new direction in fashion photography – away from airbrushed glamour and towards photorealism. The trend, however, had its darker side.

MARTIN MARGIELA
The thinking woman's designer

The Belgian designer Martin Margiela (1957–) graduated from the Royal Academy of Fine Arts in Antwerp and briefly worked as an assistant to Jean Paul Gaultier. He astounded the industry by treating fashion as an intellectual exercise, in the manner of the Japanese designer Rei Kawakubo. Calling time on the conspicuous consumption of the 1980s, he explored unconventional notions of beauty and worked in isolation, ignoring existing trends.

Margiela's uncompromising approach set him apart from his contemporaries. The unfinished seams and deconstructed shapes of a Margiela garment constantly challenged the notions of wearability. He gave catwalk presence to the humblest of materials – plastic bags, porcelain shards, even discarded car keys. In his hands, other people's rubbish became covetable again.

Experimentation did not end with his use of materials. Margiela felt that professional fashion shows had gone stale and, accordingly, held his seasonal shows in some outlandish places. From circus tents to supermarkets and subways, he invested every presentation with the frisson of the unexpected. His models were often women he had spotted in the street.

For all his industry kudos, Margiela rejected the cult of the designer, working anonymously and refusing interviews. Known as 'fashion's invisible man', he rarely had his picture taken. It was on the quality and nature of his clothes that` he wished to focus the spotlight. At the end of his shows he even took his bow as one of many team members, all dressed in identical white lab coats.

Right: Margiela's contribution to the exhibition 'Le Monde selon ses créateurs' at the Musée de la mode et du costume, Paris, 1991. Margiela's rigorously conceived clothes pushed couture deep into the realm of conceptual art.
Below: Shot of Margiela's Paris studio.

PRADA, READY-TO-WEAR 1993
Unpredictable beauty

Prada launched its ready-to-wear line in 1985 but it didn't really gain commercial traction until the 1990s. Miuccia Prada (1949–) started with simple shapes, knee-length skirts, unfussy knits and well-mannered coats. Her clothes were hardly the height of fashion: they were simply useful things made desirable by exquisite fabrics. Despite, or because of, this, her deceptively plain clothes became widely influential. As she gained confidence, Prada would revisit traditional garments, trimming nylon parkas with mink and making twin sets out of silk faille. By the middle of the decade it seemed as if the whole world was craving what *Women's Wear Daily* called 'Prada's ice-cool minimalism and deadpan eroticism'.

The designer's singular vision evolved rapidly over the decade. 'She never follows anyone else's lead, just her own original energy,' commented Julie Gilhart of Barneys department store in New York. Her ambivalence about the dictates of fashion set her apart. 'I love fashion,' Prada said, 'but I think it should stay in its place and not rule your life.' She would often focus on a silhouette or a colour she loathed because of the satisfaction it gave her when she could make something beautiful out of it. She accessorized flannel knickers with fishing waders, and once showed a raincoat that was transparent until it got wet and became opaque.

Prada elevated colours such as institutional orange, toxic green and sludgy brown to couture elegance. She used crunchy polyester, parachute nylon and stiff rayon alongside precious silks and cashmeres. She took her inspiration from 1950s pin-ups and tacky Venetian souvenirs to French haut bourgeois clothes and geek chic. The one thing that could be relied on from Prada was the fashion house's sheer unpredictability.

Miuccia Prada at the launch show of the Prada sub-brand Miu Miu, in New York, 1993. The line was so called for the designer's nickname.

ELIZABETH HURLEY IN VERSACE

A career-defining dress

The year 1994 saw the debut of 'That Dress': a sinuous, safety-pinned, neo-punk number ensured that Elizabeth Hurley (1965–) would never again be remembered simply as 'Hugh Grant's girlfriend'. In the time that it took to navigate a red carpet at London's Leicester Square, she achieved lasting fashion notoriety and was projected overnight onto the global media stage. The event was the premiere of Grant's film *Four Weddings and a Funeral*. The dress was, of course, by Gianni Versace (see pages 80–1).

The floor-length black gown was cut from silk crêpe. Its plunging neckline was secured by skinny straps that were attached to the bodice with Versace's signature gold Medusa-head buttons. The side seams were split wide open but held together with several oversized gold safety pins. There was clearly nothing between the voluptuous curves of Liz Hurley and her Versace. She managed to be both fully and barely covered. To onlookers, it seemed as if she was one deep breath away from full exposure.

'That Dress' became a Versace icon, and Hurley's debut became a memorable fashion moment for millions. When, 20 years later, Lady Gaga wore the identical dress, it was Hurley – and how much better she had looked in it – who was discussed in the gossip columns and blogs. The dress topped a poll conducted by the department store Debenhams that asked 3,000 women to select their favourite red-carpet dress. Hurley's came first, ahead of classics worn by Julia Roberts and even Audrey Hepburn.

Elizabeth Hurley is living proof of the life-changing power of the right dress on the right body at the right time. After 'That Dress', Hurley became the sex symbol of a generation.

MADCHESTER
The brilliance of 'baggy'

In the late 1980s the British charts were dominated by the sound of Duran Duran, Spandau Ballet and the pop pulp of Stock Aitken Waterman, and it seemed, as the *Guardian* stated, that 'the '80s looked destined to end in musical ignominy'. Then the 'Madchester sound' was unleashed, and packaged pop was blasted out of the cultural water as bands like The Stone Roses and Happy Mondays forged a refreshing hybrid of alternative rock, psychedelic rock and dance music.

The Stone Roses (right) helped unleash not only a new sound but a new look (below) – déclassé chic with a Manchester accent.

Manchester's Haçienda nightclub was a major catalyst, not only for the indie sound, but for the distinctive fashion look that went with it. It was a scene that was baggy by name and baggy by nature. Loose jeans (often flared), teamed with brightly coloured or tie-dyed tops, and frequently topped off with a fishing hat, as sported by Stone Roses drummer Reni, became fashionable first in Manchester and then across the whole of the UK. The look was part-hippie, part-football casual. Vintage Adidas trainers (though not just any – Samba, Forest Hills and Stan Smiths were the models of choice) were worn with tracksuit tops from sports labels like Fila and Sergio Tacchini.

Of course, this was not by any means the first time that fashions originating among working-class northern youth had become popular countrywide, but nothing had ever been picked up on by the mainstream to such a degree. For a few glorious years, Manchester, not London, defined British street style. Shami Ahmed's Manchester-based Joe Bloggs fashion label specialized in catering for the scene, and made him a multimillionaire, while brands such as Stone Island and Ralph Lauren cruised to commercial greatness off the back of the baggy look.

PIERCINGS & TATTOOS

Body art goes mainstream

In 1970 the well-known San Francisco tattooist Lyle Tuttle famously tattooed the wrist of Janis Joplin and from that moment the tattoo became an emblem of women's liberation. By the 1990s Joplin's torch of rebellion had been taken up by more and more women in the public eye. Carré Otis, Angelina Jolie and Drew Barrymore were among a number of high-profile female celebrities who unabashedly displayed their tattoos. Younger stars like Britney Spears and Christina Aguilera were quick to follow suit.

The grunge 'revolution', meanwhile, brought about an increased interest in non-mainstream music and underground scenes as well as a resurgence of punk rock. And with it came a fascination with the hallmarks of these scenes and styles: tattoos and increasingly aggressive body piercings became commonplace. Initially, these body modifications may have been a way for people to set themselves apart from the mainstream, but, as with grunge itself, it didn't take long for the mainstream to co-opt these underground fashions.

Even fashion models, those paragons of female perfection, were at it. Stefanie Seymour and Christy Turlington both had tattoos. In the beginning most models were 'inked' in places that could easily be concealed for work. Others were less bashful. Jenny Shimizu arguably launched her career when she appeared as one of the tattooed rebels in the Calvin Klein CK One campaign and proudly sported her tattoos on the runway.

By the 1990s, people with body piercings and tattoos were no longer on the fringes of society. Body art may still have had the whiff of rebellion, but it was no longer the exclusive preserve of 'bad boy' rockers and gang members.

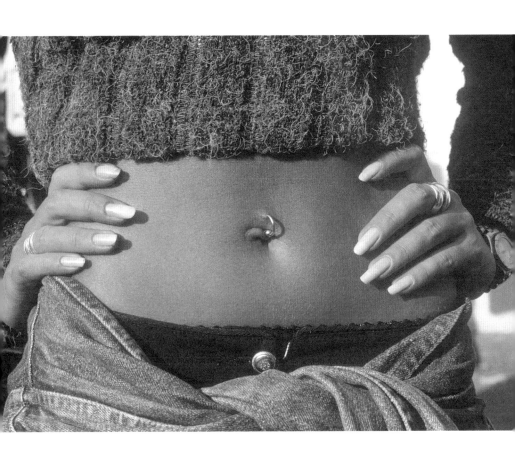

UMA THURMAN IN
PULP FICTION
The decade's *femme fatale*

One of the ultimate movie style icons of the decade was Uma Thurman (1970–), who played Mia Wallace in Quentin Tarantino's 1994 classic, *Pulp Fiction*. Mia, the wife of the terrifying mobster Marsellus Wallace, is the would-be star of a failed TV show, *Fox Force Five*, who loves cheeseburgers, luxury milkshakes, Urge Overkill, air guitar and thought experiments. She is also a substance-abusing diva who sports a lacquer-black, blunt-cut bob.

Thurman's Mia was all understated simplicity: the perfect movie icon for the minimalist decade. Her black, cropped flares and crisp white shirt, worn with a black bra and ballerina pumps, became one of the defining looks of the decade. The former model's cool blonde looks were completely transformed by the black wig, turning her into an all-too-believable mobster's moll.

Those cropped flares happened, as many of the best movie wardrobe moments do, completely by accident. While working with the film's costume designer, Betsy Heimann, the 1.8m- (6ft-) tall actress couldn't find a pair of skinny black pants with legs that were long enough. So Heimann just lopped 5cm (2in) off the hem, creating those slightly flared pedal-pushers that looked so good when Uma took to the floor with John Travolta.

Uma Thurman as Mia Wallace in Tarantino's *Pulp Fiction*. Her pared-back style of Cleopatra bob and cropped black flares made her the perfect *femme fatale* for the minimalist 1990s.

THE WONDERBRA
The decade's best supporting role

Sales of the Wonderbra had been ticking over nicely since the 1960s, when advertising for the underwired, padded cleavage-booster promised that it 'makes 34 look 36, makes 36 look pow'. In the early 1990s, the push-up properties of the Wonderbra were rediscovered by millions of curve-craving women who unabashedly wore their Wonderbras fully on display or barely hidden under mesh T-shirts or transparent blouses. (Lingerie as outerwear first became a fashion statement in 1990, when Jean Paul Gaultier designed the cone bra for Madonna's Blond Ambition Tour.)

Propelled purely by the momentum of the fashion fad, sales of the bra escalated at such a rate that, by 1993, it was estimated that one in eight of all the bras bought in the UK was a Wonderbra. The trend gathered momentum throughout the decade, with underwear being designed specifically to show under or through outerwear in eye-popping fluorescent colours and patterns and often with a matching or clashing G-string showing above the waistband of jeans or low-slung trousers.

In 1994 giant billboards went up along major roads and roundabouts featuring the model Eva Herzigova smiling down at her voluptuous Wonderbra-enhanced cleavage with the caption 'Hello Boys'. The advertisement created a sensation. Urban myth has it that traffic flow slowed and car accidents increased around the location of the billboard sites. The cause was attributed to (male) drivers being distracted by the advertisements. Afterwards, there was a call for all large billboards to be subject to planning permission.

Pop star Simon Le Bon and actress Amanda de Cadenet at the Herb Ritts exhibition at the Hamiltons Gallery, London. The Wonderbra rode high on the 1990s trend for visible underwear.

'THE RACHEL'
The hairstyle of the 1990s

In the 1990s hairdressers all over the world had to grapple with their clients' descriptions of the 'Rachel Cut'. Conversations in salons from Sidney to San Francisco opened something like this: 'So I'd like it a bit tousled, with some body, but not curly, because I'd like it smooth and sort of shoulder length or maybe a bit shorter, with sort of layers, and I'd like it brown but with blonde highlights … Make that lowlights and a bit straight but with the ends turned under and some turned out … You know what I mean?'

What they were getting at was the bouncy layered hairstyle popularized by Jennifer Aniston in Season One of the hit American sitcom *Friends* and named after her character, Rachel Green. Rachel wore that haircut for the first two seasons of the sitcom – enough time for women all over the world to succumb to a hairdressing trend that reached epidemic proportions and which soon became known simply as 'The Rachel'.

Throughout the twentieth century, female icons have been defined by their hair. There was Brigitte Bardot's beehive, Farrah Fawcett's windswept mane, Audrey Hepburn's chignon and Twiggy's bob. At times, it seems almost as if their personalities have become overshadowed by their iconic locks. It turns out that Aniston is a case in point. In an interview with *Allure* magazine, she admitted to hating 'The Rachel', confessing, 'I love Chris [McMillan, her hairstylist] [… but] I think it was the ugliest haircut I've ever seen.'

Jennifer Aniston sports 'The Rachel' – a haircut as redolent of the 1990s as Farrah Fawcett's flick was of the 1980s.

ALICIA SILVERSTONE IN *CLUELESS*

Teen queen in tartan

For a generation of teenagers, Alicia Silverstone (1976–) defined 1990s style. Or, rather, her fashion-fabulous character Cher Horowitz did, in the classic film of the decade *Clueless* (1995). The movie opens with our heroine going through her computer-organized wardrobe trying to find an outfit before class. And, in that moment, millions of adolescent girls wished they could be her. The plaid skirts, the berets, those sunglasses!

The movie-going public fell instantly in love with the ditzy Beverly Hills fashion victim. With the exception of Silverstone, that is. On first reading writer-director Amy Heckerling's script, the young actress was dumbfounded. 'I thought, "Who is this girl?" I had nothing in common with her at all. I thought she was a materialistic, annoying little bitch.'

Clueless is remembered for its slang ('Going postal'; 'Like, whatever!') but also for its style, which continued to ignite trends throughout the decade. The navy blazer, knitted tank top over poplin shirt and miniskirt ensemble was a classic Cher look, as was a button-down white cotton shirt, an argyle or plaid miniskirt, knee-high white socks and silver Mary Janes.

Silverstone's character won over the most cynical fashion viewer when, mugged at gunpoint in a parking lot, she protests that her dress was by the 'totally important designer … it's an Alaïa!'. In the panoply of fashion muggings, it is equalled only by Carrie's brave effort to save her Manolos from a thief in *Sex and the City*.

Clueless will forever be burned on the retinas of teenage girls as a blur of flamboyant tartans: reportedly, more than 50 different plaid patterns were used for the movie's wardrobe.

LAURYN HILL
Keeping it real

In the early 1990s Lauryn Hill (1975–) made her name as an actress and as the lead singer with the Fugees, whose cover version (1995) of Roberta Flack's 'Killing Me Softly' became part of tho coundtraok to tho dooado. Thon, in 1008, Hill roloacod her solo debut album, *The Miseducation of Lauryn Hill*, and she became the first woman and hip-hop artist to win five Grammy Awards, receiving the honours for Album of the Year, Best New Arlisl, Besl Female R&B Performance, Besl R&B Sorig, for 'Doo Wop (That Thing)', and Best R&B Album. Her future success seemed assured.

Hill was an undoubted talent, but it was her flawless and, crucially, dark-skinned looks that attracted the most attention, along with a style that was glamorous and street, Hollywood and hip-hop, in equal measures. Her succession of Afro hairstyles drew particular comment and inspired a whole generation of young black women. In an industry where 'natural' African hair had once again become a no-no, her preference for kinky curls and cute dreadlocks was a breath of fresh air.

Hill's record company, Columbia, invested heavily in her follow-up album, but the pressure to submit to the image machine proved too much for the singer. Rightly or wrongly, Hill interpreted Columbia's actions as exploitation and, for a time, she disappeared from the industry altogether. *The Miseducation* remains her only solo studio album to date.

Lauryn Hill with the Fugees in 1995. Her Nefertiti-like beauty and savvy style were the perfect foil to the hip-hop vibe.

JIL SANDER

The new woman

The German designer Jil Sander (1943–) led the way in the minimalist fashion movement that began in the 1990s. Preferring to work in a largely monochromatic colour palette, she strove constantly to perfect construction and eradicate extraneous seaming and detailing. Popularizing the unlined, soft-shoulder jacket, she fitted in perfectly with the 1990s, a time when women sought some quiet respite from the flamboyant 1980s. 'Initially, it was the unpractical in fashion that brought me to design my own line,' she said. 'I felt that it was much more attractive to cut clothes with respect for the living, three-dimensional body rather than to cover the body with decorative ideas.'

In white shirt and black suit, Sander dressed a woman in touch with a new kind of power. The woman who came of age in the 1990s was not like her sisters in the 1980s who tried to make their mark by expanding their shoulders. They were also quite different from Rei Kawakubo's woman who haughtily rejected old-style femininity. Sander's woman was not afraid either to wear a dress or to dress like a man, as long as she was wearing luxury fabrics. Detractors called it 'lesbian chic'.

Key instruments in her success were the team Sander gathered around her to create the image that cemented her position as the 'Queen of Less'. The art director Marc Ascoli engineered the look of both her fashion shows and her advertising imagery, while Nick Knight was outstanding among the prestigious photographers she and Ascoli hired.

Tatjana Patitz in an advertising image shot by Nick Knight and art-directed by Marc Ascoli for Jil Sander's Spring/ Summer 1992 collection.

GRACE CODDINGTON

Power broker with a light touch

Grace Coddington (1941–), the creative director of American *Vogue*, burst into the wider public consciousness as the unexpected breakout star of *The September Issue*, the 2009 documentary about the production of the September 2007 issue of American *Vogue*. Although she had long been a towering figure in the industry, she was relatively unknown outside fashion circles. Yet she and Anna Wintour (see pages 106–7) deserve equal credit for the cultural monolith that is American *Vogue*. As creative director, it is from her imagination that the magic and romance of the magazine spring.

After retiring from modelling in the late 1960s, Coddington took a job at British *Vogue*, an operation she remembers as far more amateurish and casual than its American counterpart. 'The solution to most problems was,' she recalls, '"Mmmm, let's have a nice cup of tea."' She quickly moved up the ranks to become photo editor before moving to New York in the 1980s, working first for Calvin Klein and then rejoining her old colleague Wintour at American *Vogue*. It was there that she created some of the iconic shoots of the 1990s, the hallmark of her work being an astonishing attention to detail. 'Everything has to be perfect,' she has said. 'You can't just fudge it. […]To do things right takes a lot of work. […] Life is tough. You have to work really hard, long hours.'

It is easy to see Coddington and Wintour as the heart and brain of American *Vogue*. Over the years they have settled into a kind of yin–yang relationship. Coddington dresses in minimalist black; Wintour wears fur and diamonds. Wintour peppers her magazine with the famous; Coddington tends to disdain Hollywood actors and their publicity entourages. They both fiercely champion the designers they love. Coddington's favourites include Marc Jacobs (pages 46–7), Miuccia Prada (pages 52–3), John Galliano (pages 86–7) and Helmut Lang (pages 84–5), all of whom rose to prominence in the 1990s.

Grace Coddington – until recently the unsung heroine of American *Vogue*.

MARIO TESTINO

The power behind the big brands

Mario Testino's big career break came in 1995, courtesy of Madonna. The singer was supposed to be taking part in an advertising campaign for Versace, with the great Richard Avedon as the photographer. Instead, having spotted the relative unknown in a magazine, she urged her friend Gianni Versace (see pages 80–1) to book Mario Testino (1954–) instead. When the pictures came out, Versace decided to give the photographer a headlining credit. It was, however, while working with Carine Roitfeld, consultant to Tom Ford (see pages 76–7) at Gucci, that Testino truly went stellar.

Together, they unleashed a campaign of such sizzling sexuality that it would define the look of the end of the millennium. With his images for Gucci, Testino called time on the nihilism of 'heroin chic'. Before Roitfeld, Testino (who had moved to London from Lima in the 1970s) had been an enchanted Anglophile whose work channelled the charm and formality of Cecil Beaton and Norman Parkinson. With Roitfeld, his style took on a new hard-edged glamour, creating glossy, seductive advertising images that would be instrumental in launching the phenomenon of the fashion label as a global superbrand.

Testino's career high point came when he was chosen by Princess Diana for her *Vanity Fair* photoshoot in 1997, which turned out to be her last sitting. The pictures were the most intimate ever taken of Diana, showing her at her most informal and – with prescient irony – her most vulnerable.

Mario Testino's powerful visual style helped to define the new age of the global superbrand.

TOM FORD AT GUCCI

1996

'Sexing up' luxury

Gucci, the apogee of Italian luxury in the 1960s and '70s, was suffering from a blight of bad licences and dwindling into faded glory when its new creative director, Dawn Mello, snapped up the eager young designer Tom Ford (1961–) and appointed him as the Gucci's women's ready-to-wear designer in 1990. The house was in such bad shape that it looked like it might go under at any time and Ford, Mello recalls, was practically the only candidate for the job.

Ford had been an art history student at New York University and had also trained as an actor. His university career ended abruptly after a year, eclipsed by the distractions of Studio 54 and Andy Warhol's Factory, a lifestyle he financed with acting and modelling. He subsequently enrolled at The New Parsons School for Design, studying interior architecture, before finally transferring to fashion. By the end of the 1980s he was working under Marc Jacobs (see pages 46–7), who was design director at Perry Ellis.

Dawn Mello's call from Milan was Ford's big break. In 1994, following Mello's departure, Ford was promoted to creative director. It was at this point that the years spent carousing, posing and people-watching in New York finally delivered. Ford's Gucci explored the glamorous limits of those disco years: with velvet hip-hugging jeans, skinny satin shirts and high-shine patent boots, or sinuous jersey dresses, notched-lapel jackets and over-the-knee boots. Echoes of Halston and Giorgio di Sant' Angelo were not lost on the house's now-burgeoning clientele, in thrall to the new sexed-up Gucci.

To elaborate on the Gucci story, Ford enlisted the help of stylist Carine Roitfeld and photographer Mario Testino (see pages 74–5). Together, they created international advertising campaigns that reflected Gucci's new-found fashion power and which often, in their unabashed sensual appeal, courted outright controversy.

Tom Ford is credited with transforming Italian fashion house Gucci into a global superbrand, creating clothes that were at once erotically charged and sleekly sophisticated.

TOMMY HILFIGER
The new all-American

In the mid-1980s Tommy Hilfiger (1951–) undertook a public relations assault on the fashion firmament. He had no fashion background to speak of, but, in 1985, a huge billboard appeared in New York's Times Square alluding to Tommy Hilfiger as a great American menswear designer. Branded as fashion's great pretender at the time, he was likened by the industry to The Monkees, the prefabricated pop group of the 1960s modelled after The Beatles.

Ralph Lauren was Hilfiger's role model, and the newcomer followed the designer's every move. Lauren had cornered the market in the aesthetic of the patrician WASP, while Calvin Klein owned sex. Hilfiger spotted a niche for the clean-scrubbed romance of Middle America. His ads featured groups of young models at 4th of July barbecues, soccer games and downtown parades. Hilfiger simultaneously reinvented himself as a fashion celebrity. He went out on the road doing back-to-back store appearances, posing for pictures and signing autographs. His regional road shows were the perfect opportunity to check out what the coolest kids all over the country were wearing. He came back to New York and had his team of designers make sure that they were catered to.

Hilfiger was blessed with street sense, a common touch and happy timing. With the arrival of the information age, America embraced a lifestyle outfitted in casualwear, and Hilfiger was ready to step up. He was the first to plaster his name on rugby shirts and tops, winning him a place alongside Puma, Adidas and Gucci in the rappers' wardrobes. He understood the power of rap culture, a genre that the fashion industry couldn't, or wouldn't, relate to.

Hilfiger may have started out as a Ralph copycat but in the 1990s he was doing his own thing: a hybrid mix of preppy and street. In 1996 the Council of Fashion Designers of America voted him the best menswear designer.

Tommy Hilfiger crafted an all-American look that walked the fine line between preppy and street, cool and kitsch.

GIANNI VERSACE
The last emperor

Gianni Versace (1946–97) redefined the codes of elegance in the 1990s, though for him the lure of excess never lost its appeal. A Versace collection glorified the human form, enveloping it in an orgy of colour, print, embroidery and decoration. He dazzled at all times with the fearlessness of each new style statement, but he also drew huge respect for his mastery of his craft. The rich silk prints made by artisans in Como, the embroideries realized by craftsmen in Paris and the faultless tailoring and construction that was produced by his team in Milan may not have been exactly to everyone's taste, but his clothes were always impeccably made.

Versace embraced every aspect of an industry that was undergoing rapid globalization. He quickly recognized the power of branding and put his stamp not just on clothes but on perfumes, cosmetics, watches and home furnishings. He was a media darling, his accessibility and openness rivalled only by that other great communicator Karl Lagerfeld. In addition, he pioneered the use of the Internet to complement the traditional media coverage of runway shows in New York, Paris, Milan and London. It was all about global communication.

Celebrity, too, was key, and Versace courted the flashiest stars – Sylvester Stallone, Tina Turner and Elizabeth Hurley. But Versace also got in touch with people of more dubious reputation, once boasting that the rapper Tupac Shakur was wearing Versace both on the day he went into prison and on the day he was discharged. Fashion connoisseurs loved to quip that the wives of wealthy men wore Armani but their mistresses preferred Versace.

The media-savvy Versace knew how to put on a show, hiring the best photographers and legions of supermodels.

JFK, JR. & CAROLYN BESSETTE 1996
The world's most beautiful couple

In 1989 Carolyn Bessette (1966–99) joined Calvin Klein's PR department (see pages 34–5), where she attended to the requests of journalists and helped dress the likes of socialite Blaine Trump and news presenter Diane Sawyer. It was Kelly Klein, Calvin's wife, who introduced her to the American socialite and lawyer John F. Kennedy, Jr (1960–99).

Bessette was the embodiment of modern beauty. Although JFK, Jr. had dated Sarah Jessica Parker, Daryl Hannah and even, briefly, Madonna, Bessette was the one of whom it was whispered, 'Jackie would have approved.' She had timeless style. She carried the Hermès Birkin bag long before Victoria Beckham amassed her million-dollar collection. Her wardrobe reflected an industry insider's appreciation of fashion: Yohji Yamamoto, Prada, Manolo Blahnik, Miu Miu and, of course, Calvin Klein were the key labels. Bessette often dressed in black, the New York fashionistas' favourite colour.

She was rarely seen without the bold, red lipstick on her otherwise bare face, and her long blonde hair was either pulled back or worn straight. With a public aloofness that was invariably interpreted as 'mystique', Bessette had magazine and newspaper editors lining up for photoshoots and interviews.

The couple married in a secret ceremony on Cumberland Island, Georgia in September 1996, in a tiny, wind-battered wooden church. For her wedding dress, Bessette turned to her former colleague and friend from her Calvin Klein days, Narciso Rodriguez.

The marriage of John F. Kennedy, Jr. and Carolyn Bessette seemed almost to be a second incarnation of the Kennedy–Bouvier relationship of the 1960s. Tragically, both husband and wife were killed in a plane accident in 1999.

HELMUT LANG
Ice-cool minimalism

The founding father of 1990s fashion minimalism was Helmut Lang (1956–). The Austrian designer was influenced not only by modernist architecture, but also by German expressionism and by Vienna, the city where, at the age of 23, he first set up his business. Lang, a business student and fashion autodidact, began by making made-to-measure clothes out of a small studio but he soon relocated to Paris, after presenting his work as part of an exhibition at the Centre Pompidou. In 1997 he would move camp once more, this time to New York City.

In his high-minded intellectualism, Lang has often been compared to Rei Kawakubo and Yohji Yamamoto, though he has always been easier to wear than these innovative Japanese designers. Commercially, he enjoyed a huge success, especially in his New York phase. He rewrote the codes not only of the modern woman's wardrobe but the modern man's as well. The photographer Elfie Semotan, one of Lang's closest friends and a frequent collaborator, has said of him: 'He taught men how to look cool and elegant without looking like they had thought too much about their clothes.' Meanwhile, Lang also forged links between fashion and the art world, collaborating with artists such as Jenny Holzer and Louise Bourgeois, and frequently used art imagery in his advertising.

At the opening of a retrospective at the Bath Museum of Fashion, its curator, Rosemary Harden, wrote, 'Helmut Lang is the antithesis of the red-carpet celebrity dressing of the past 10 years. […] He has a very specific aesthetic, it is very pared down; there aren't frills and bows and ruffles.' Lang is, for many, the last of the great couturiers. With his chic white dresses and sleek trouser suits, Lang's meticulous designs were the perfect encapsulation of the 1990s credo of 'less is more'.

Simplicity and functionality: Helmut Lang injected fashion with a cleansing dose of Bauhaus-inspired modernism.

The decade got off to a peripatetic start for London's brightest fashion star. John Galliano (1960–) had a big reputation, matched only by the size of his overdraft. Faycal Amor, his latest backer, had cut ties, and, adrift in Paris – or so fashion legend has it Galliano was surviving on baked beans cooked on a burner and by scrounging a bed for the night from friends.

Enter Anna Wintour (see pages 106–7), a knight in shining Chanel and Manolos. In 1993 she introduced him to Sao Schlumberger, a socialite of fabled wealth and with a couture wardrobe to match. In 1994, in Schlumberger's empty *hôtel particulier* by the Jardin du Luxembourg in Paris, he showed a capsule collection of 17 looks all made from the same bolts of black cloth, the only material he could afford. The invitation was a rusty key with a handwritten label attached. Models Kate Moss, Linda Evangelista and Christy Turlington all walked for free as a favour to their old friend. It was a great fashion moment. Once more, the press, store buyers and fashionable women beat a path to the Galliano studio, a singularly unglamorous place in the as yet not quite fashionable Bastille.

The show began Galliano's upturn in fortune. In 1995 LVMH appointed him head designer at Givenchy and then, barely two years later at Christian Dior – the ultimate prize. His couture debut collection in January 1997 in the Grand Hôtel was theatrical yet reverent. The ballroom was transformed into a Dior salon with 800m (875 yds) of the house's signature grey fabric and 4,000 roses. The first 17 outfits had names that were variations on the founder's name, such as Diorbella, Diorla,… but this was no simple homage. Along with Dior signatures such as the hound's-tooth checks and white lace, there were evening dresses in sinuous Boldini-esque silhouettes, oriental embroideries and whimsical accessories such as Masai collars. It was Dior, but reinvented.

Encore Dior... Galliano's reinvention of the Dior look teamed figure-hugging silhouettes with gorgeous orientalist *jeux d'esprit.* This transparent, topless dress from the Autumn-Winter 1997 collection took the style to its limit.

KRISTEN McMENAMY

A true fashion original

In the 1990s there was a shift away from the glamour that had so obsessed fashion in the 1980s towards a more unconventional take on beauty. Kristen McMenamy (1966–) spearheaded this developing trend, able to transform, with apparent ease, from classic *jolie laide* to unvarnished anti-fashion icon to head-turning beauty. This, together with her powerful personality and tenacity in pursuit of 'the perfect picture', made her one of the most fascinating fashion professionals of the decade.

McMenamy's breakthrough moment came in 1990 when she landed one of fashion's most prestigious ad campaigns working for the German designer Jil Sander. Within a few fashion seasons, she was also the face of Prada, Moschino, Chanel, Armani and Versace. In 1992, another transformative year, she was featured, alongside Naomi Campbell and Nadja Auermann, in a fashion story shot by Steven Meisel (see pages 14–15) for American *Vogue*. 'Grunge and Glory' was a celebration of the subculture that had become fashion's latest fixation and defined a shift in the mood of the decade. McMenamy's elevation to the pantheon of supermodels was assured.

McMenamy's startling, androgynous looks represented a shift away from the bland glamour of the 1980s towards idiosyncrasy and individualism. 'I represent the individual,' the model has said. 'I represent being happy with who you are.'

SPICE GIRLS

Girl power goes global

In the summer of 1996 the Spice Girls released their debut single 'Wannabe' in the UK, and the music journalist Paul Gorman wrote, 'Just when boys with guitars threaten to rule pop life – an all-girl pop group have arrived with enough sass to burst that rockist bubble.' The song stayed at Number 1 for seven weeks, becoming the biggest-selling single by an all-female group of all time. In October 1996 they were the star turn at the British Fashion Awards.

At the heart of their success was the marketability of their image and their willingness to exploit it in an age that was increasingly media driven. The Spice Girls became icons of 1990s fashion, too. Victoria Adams – or 'Posh Spice', as she was dubbed – was known for her choppy brunette bob hairstyle and love of designer labels. Geri Halliwell – called Ginger Spice because of her 'liveliness, zest, and flaming red hair' – became notorious for her outrageous stage outfits. Her Union Jack dress was one of the most copied frocks of the decade.

Girl power took the world by storm. A ridiculously successful second album, *Spiceworld* (1997), continued the momentum, and by the time of the release of the single 'Spice up Your Life' there was barely a billboard or TV screen on the planet that did not have their faces on it: a phenomenon they themselves parodied in the song's video, which shows the band flying around in a spaceship in a 'universe' of advertisements featuring their faces. The fashion industry was alert to the burgeoning trend and soon the high street was awash with platform shoes, minidresses and leopard prints.

Posh, Baby, Scary, Ginger and Sporty: while they may not have embodied everything about the 1990s woman, the Spice Girls didn't just take part in 1990s culture, they *made* it. Worldwide, the phrase 'girl power' became a byword for the growing confidence of young women everywhere.

COOL BRITANNIA

British style blooms again

'Cool Britannia' was the moniker given to the surge of national pride in UK culture that secured enormous global influence for the country in the late 1990s. Tony Blair's Labour government came to power in 1997 on a platform of modernization, with its election theme song urging the electorate to believe that 'Things can only get better'.

Since 1994, Britain's National Lottery had been pumping capital into the arts. The Young British Artists had made London a hot spot for art and design: some London art dealers and collectors, such as Jay Jopling and Charles Saatchi, were more famous than their artists, and most artists were more famous than their art. The launch of magazines such as *Loaded* and *Dazed & Confused* at home and the eminence of British ex-pats such as Anna Wintour and Liz Tilberis in New York had made London, once again, the focus of the global cool hunters' attention. There was a resurgence of a distinctive British sound from bands such as Oasis, Blur and Suede. The Spice Girls (see pages 90– 1) were the most successful all-female pop group ever.

In the fashion world, Central Saint Martins College of Arts and Design was the globally acknowledged centre of excellence. London Fashion Week was surfing a wave of new talent, and in those heady days even the lofty Paris fashion houses were not immune to the pull of British talent. The luxury conglomerate LVMH installed Saint Martins graduates John Galliano (see pages 86–7) and Alexander McQueen (see pages 100–1) at the couture houses of Christian Dior and Givenchy, respectively. Ralph Lauren, Louis Vuitton, Gucci, Calvin Klein (see pages 34–5), Donna Karan and Tommy Hilfiger (see pages 78–9) all grappled for flagship stores on London's Bond Street.

Unfortunately, Cool Britannia was to suffer a near-fatal chill when, in 1998, *The Economist* was among several august publications that noted that 'many people are already sick of the phrase'. By 2000 the fickle world of fashion had moved on and the moniker was being used mainly in a mocking or ironic way.

Meg Matthews and Noel Gallagher pose outside 10 Downing Street during Prime Minister Tony Blair's famous 'Cool Britannia' party. It could be argued that the UK pop 'renaissance' of the 1990s was at least in part a media creation.

BRITISH MILLINERY

Getting ahead in hats

The 1980s and '90s saw the meteoric rise of British millinery. In the space between the era when no polite lady would have dared leave the house bareheaded, through the 1970s, when a hat was anathema to the jeans-wearing population, hats struggled on the sidelines of mainstream style. The peacock parade that was street fashion in the 1980s changed everything. By the end of the 1990s Britain led the field in fashion millinery, and the two men behind its resurgence were Stephen Jones (1957–) and Philip Treacy (1967–).

Jones first made a name for himself with the hats he created for Boy George when both were habitués of London's Blitz Club. Jones went on to work with Jean Paul Gaultier and Vivienne Westwood (he created her iconic Harris Tweed Crown of 1987) and since 1993 he has been part of the team that works with John Galliano.

Treacy graduated from the Royal College of Art in 1990 and, having come under the wing of Isabella Blow (see pages 104–5), set up a workshop in the basement of her house in Belgravia. Treacy's career has never known anything but top gear, starting as it did with collaborations with Karl Lagerfeld at Chanel, Versace, Valentino and Ralph Lauren. In 2000 he became the first milliner to have his own couture show during Paris Fashion Week.

While hats have always been the default option for designers in need of a show-stopping statement, the British milliners' greatest achievement lies in the fact that they reintroduced hats to the wardrobes of ordinary women. It is debatable whether, even with their unique talents, either Jones or Treacy could have flourished anywhere else but in London. Their work has always been the perfect complement to the national nonconformist style. As Jones has said, 'The hat is a certain British thing that people do love wearing.'

Above: The star British milliner Philip Treacy prepares the singer Grace Jones for a fashion shoot. Below: A shot from the Treacy-Jones shoot. By the 1990s, hats had regained their starring role in fashion, adding a final flourish of drama and spectacle.

THE ANTWERP SIX

A new world view

After the Japanese, the next wave of newcomers to completely change the fashion landscape came from Belgium. They first alighted in London, in 1986, choosing to show as part of London Fashion Week as the 'Antwerp Six'. Fellow graduates from the Academy of Fine Arts in Antwerp, they had all established businesses at home but were struggling for international recognition. Propelled by Belgian government grants, Dries Van Noten (1958–), Ann Demeulemeester (1959–), Dirk Bikkembergs (1959–), Walter Van Beirendonck (1957–), Dirk Van Saene (1959–) and Marina Yee (1958–) set out to conquer Europe.

By the early 1990s they had all moved to Paris and were among the hottest tickets on the Chambre Syndicale's schedule. They fascinated with their innovative take on luxury, distinguished by its powerful combination of austerity, utility and perfectionism. Their vision took Japanese deconstruction to its next natural step, breaking down the traditional elements of a garment and creating new silhouettes. 'We were ready to change the world,' remembers Ann Demeulemeester. 'People no longer chose clothes as a disguise. They chose them to express something. That's the whole difference between the 1980s and the 1990s. They no longer used clothes to impress other people – they used them to feel good about themselves.'

The original Antwerp Six would be joined over the course of the decade by Haider Ackermann, Veronique Branquinho, Raf Simons and Olivier Theyskens. They showed they were adept at developing their own labels and making them commercial without compromising their creative dynamic. 'I already thought there were too many clothes in the world and I shouldn't add to them,' said Demeulemeester. 'I could only add something that hadn't already been made.'

Dries Van Noten's cool, deconstructed elegance: ready-to-wear, Spring/ Summer 1998, Paris. The group of Belgian designers managed to marry intellectual ambition with marketability.

HUSSEIN CHALAYAN
Fashion as conceptual art

The only child of Turkish Cypriot parents, Hussein Chalayan (1970–) was born in Nicosia, Cyprus, and lived between the island and London. 'As a child, I would go from Cyprus, a more desolate place, a culture which has seen two wars, to London where, suddenly, there was everything, and then back again,' he has said. 'That allowed me to process any information, to contemplate things and develop any ideas in between.'

When he graduated from Central Saint Martins College of Arts and Design in 1993, global attention was on London's creative scene, though not yet on its fashion. It was Brit Pop and Brit Art that were on the rise. Chalayan and Alexander McQueen (see pages 100–1), who had graduated from Saint Martins the year before, had to battle for recognition. With hindsight, both men had one important thing in common: the desire to create a universe beyond the conventions of the catwalk.

One piece from Chalayan's graduate collection sums up the aesthetic of this most conceptual of all fashion designers – a simple dress that he had sprinkled with iron filings and buried in a friend's back garden, leaving it to moulder into its elegantly decayed final state. In the context of the conventional 'sketch, cut, sew and show' of the fashion industry, his unique creative processes explain his status as one of commercial fashion's most intriguing outsiders. Part-organic, part-technical, part-scientific, part-archaeological, Chalayan's way of working not only defines him; it also sets him apart.

Chalayan's compelling originality makes him fashion's most authentic postmodernist. Constantly re-examining accepted techniques and forms, his approach is often political in nature and inspired by diverse subjects such as science, sculpture, technology and architecture. He is at once simple and organic and highly technical – a paradox evident, for example, in the fibreglass dress that mimicked the mechanics of an aeroplane wings or the famous table skirt of the 'Afterwords' collection (2000).

Shot from the 'Geotropics' collection, Spring/ Summer 1999. In this dress incorporating a chair Hussein Chalayan evokes one of his enduring themes – the condition of the immigrant in perpetual transit between cultures and nations.

ALEXANDER McQUEEN

British fashion genius

1999

In 1992 Lee Alexander McQueen (1969–2010) graduated from London's Central Saint Martins College of Arts and Design with a collection provocatively entitled 'Jack the Ripper Stalks His Victims'. From the outset, McQueen was a designer with a singular and consistent point of view, laying down the signature ingredients that would persist throughout his career: notably his fascination with the Victorian Gothic, his passion for narrative, and his penchant for the tailored silhouette.

In the audience of his graduate show was stylist Isabella Blow (see pages 104–5) who, legend has it, bought every piece he had and adopted him as her protégé. In the four years that followed his graduation, McQueen gathered the team who would remain his trusted circle until his suicide in 2010. In 1994 Katy England became his creative director; in 1996 Sarah Burton headed up his design team; and that same year Sam Gainsbury joined the group as show producer.

In those days, Gainsbury was lucky to have £600 to foot the bill – their last project together ran to a budget of six figures. Regardless of budget, however, McQueen shows were produced on a lavish, theatrical scale, courting both wonder and shock in equal measure. In 1998 double amputee model Aimee Mullins took centre stage, striding down the catwalk on intricately carved wooden legs. Later that year Shalom Harlow closed the show in a strapless white dress, rotating slowly on a platform in a hypnotic dance as two giant robotic arms sprayed her with paint.

In 1996, after only eight seasons showing his own label, McQueen joined Givenchy, replacing John Galliano (see pages 86–7). It was always an awkward relationship and he stayed with the French fashion house for barely five years, when the contract that he said was 'constraining his creativity' came to an end. From there, he went into partnership with the Gucci Group – a move that enabled his fashion house to develop into a global brand.

The McQueen at Givenchy Autumn/Winter 1999/2000 show, 'The Overlook', was inspired by Stanley Kubrick's movie masterpiece *The Shining* (1980). The catwalk became a Narnia-like world of falling snow and barren trees, through which the models ice-skated in luxurious furs, full-length coats and elaborate swan-like dresses.

GWYNETH PALTROW

Redefining the glacial blonde

After both starring in *Se7en* (1995), Gwyneth Paltrow (1972–) and Brad Pitt became the most beautiful couple in Hollywood. It was inconceivable that, thereafter, she would go unnoticed. Add some award worthy screen performances – *Emma* (1996), *Sliding Doors* (1998) and *A Perfect Murder* (1998) – and Paltrow established her very own legions of dedicated fans, hooked on her talent and style. The pinnacle of her decade was the Academy Award she won for Best Actress for her performance in *Shakespeare in Love* (1998).

Paltrow at the 1999 Academy Awards. Her acceptance speech was as famous for her tears as for her Ralph Lauren cottoncandy-pink gown.

To accept the award, she wore a pink Ralph Lauren gown. This split the critics. *Vogue* may have gushed about 'Ralph Lauren's melting pink paper taffeta prom gown with Harry Winston diamonds', but even Blythe Danner, the star's own mother, admitted that, 'it didn't fit very well'. Nonetheless, Paltrow still managed to set off a trend for pink – a flotilla of cottoncandy princess dresses was launched in its wake.

Paltrow is not a fashion leader, as she herself admits. One of her greatest fashion influences, she once confessed to *Vogue*, was the uniform of her smart school on New York's Upper East Side: 'You have to wear this very posh, clean outfit every day – your white shirt and little grey kilt, and put it with black eyeliner or whatever. It's a great look.' Nonetheless, designers enthusiastically embraced her. Her all-American style was a perfect canvas – whether for Ralph Lauren's clean-cut, upper-crust clothes or for Calvin Klein's vision of minimalist perfection.

With her lean frame and blonde hair, it was almost inevitable that comparisons would be made with Grace Kelly, particularly after Paltrow's role in *A Perfect Murder*, the remake of the Hitchcock vehicle for Kelly, *Dial M for Murder*. Her patrician presence in *The Talented Mr. Ripley* (1999) secured her position as Kelly's heir in the style stakes. Gwyneth Paltrow herself has never admitted to having pretensions to the crown, summing up the style that rivets millions of magazine readers as simply 'preppy'.

ISABELLA BLOW

Irrepressible style seeker

Isabella Blow (1958–2007) played the most ill-defined and under-appreciated role in the realm of fashion creation – that of a muse. Her extraordinary wardrobe fascinated fashion fans worldwide. She was photographed wherever she went, courted by street photographers and fashion superstars alike. To many, she epitomized the English eccentric. She earned a living as a fashion editor (*Tatler*, *The Sunday Times*) and as creative consultant to commercial companies, such as Swarovski, whose budgets were able to stretch to her expenses.

Most of all, however, Blow was a discoverer and nurturer of raw fashion talent. She assembled a family of fashion foundlings around her, all of whom were singularly talented. Many of them got their first big break thanks to her, and some are indebted to her for their entire careers. Among them were the milliner Philip Treacy (see pages 94–5) and the designer Alexander McQueen (see pages 100–1). She worked with Julien Macdonald and Hussein Chalayan (see pages 98–9). She was also a formative force in the fledgling careers of photographers such as Juergen Teller, Alastair Thain and Sean Ellis, and models including Sophie Dahl, Stella Tennant and Honor Fraser.

Blow's provocative image both buttressed and concealed a fragile personality. She once admitted that 'if I am feeling really low, I go and see Philip [Treacy], cover my face and feel fantastic'. In his biography, Blow's husband of 18 years, Detmar, wrote about how clothes were both 'armour' and 'a distraction for a woman fighting with inner demons'. Few outsiders knew how severe was Blow's depression – she committed suicide in 2007 at the age of 48.

Both armour and distraction: Isabella Blow's inimitable fashion sense attracted curiosity, wonder and the occasional sneer.

ANNA WINTOUR
Fashion's unflappable queen

In 1988, in a bid to revitalize its ailing flagship title, the Condé Nast bosses lured Anna Wintour (1949–) to New York to be editor of American *Vogue*. The 'Anna-effect' was immediate. She marked out her territory in no uncertain terms with her first cover. Out went the toothsome close-up shots taken in an artificially lit studio and in came the relaxed but glamorous lifestyle 'scenes'. The November 1988 issue featured the 19-year-old Israeli model Michaela Bercu strolling down a New York street, with beach hair, a big smile, a pair of distressed Guess jeans and a jewelled Christian Lacroix couture jacket.

Wintour established herself as a risk taker, with limited patience for the customary ways of doing things, a keen sense of the commercial, an instinct for the *zeitgeist* and a feeling for fashion that influenced the way millions of women dressed. She proved herself a proactive supporter of designers, too, supporting fledgling talents such as Marc Jacobs as enthusiastically as she endorsed established titans such as Karl Lagerfeld, Oscar de la Renta and Gianni Versace (see pages 80–1). Under Wintour's watch, photographers, makeup artists, models and hairstylists all got credits on the fashion pages.

Her friends say it is her shyness that is behind her reputation for being haughty and aloof, although her 'Nuclear Wintour' nickname has become as emblematic as her bob and sunglasses. In the 1990s her style was still in its early evolutionary stages. Back then, though with an unmistakable leaning towards the glamorous, she had a strong sporty streak that featured fur-trimmed parkas, T-shirts and even, on occasion, jeans. Rarely seen with a handbag (even then), there was more of a ready smile and less of the enigmatic smoulder.

A classic Wintour look, with the glamour countered by the anonymity provided by the bob and sunglasses.

INDEX

PICTURE CREDITS

The publisher would like to thank the following contributors for their kind permission to reproduce the following photographs:

2 Julio Donoso/Sygma/Corbis; 4 Michel Arnaud/Corbis; 5 below Ron Galella Collection/Getty; above Stefan Rousseau/Press Association Images; 7 Michel Arnaud/Corbis; 9 Courtesy Nike; 10 SNAP/Rex Features; 11 KPA Movie Stills Library/Eyevine; 13 Tim Roney/Getty Images; 15 Ron Galella Ltd/WireImage/Getty Images; 17 Corrine Day/Trunk Archive; 19 Janette Beckman/PYMCA; 21 Rex Features; 23 Chris Moore/Catwalking; 25 below Steve Back/Daily Mail/Rex Features above Dana Lixenberg/Corbis; 27 Mark Large/Daily Mail/Rex Features; 29 Richard Melloul/Sygma/Corbis; 31 Jens Mortensen/The New York Times Syndicate; 33 Lyn Goldsmith/Corbis; 35 LFI; 37 Advertising Archives; 38 PYMCA 39 Matthew Smith/PYMCA; 41 Courtesy Art Club 2000; 43 Andre Camara/Reuters/Corbis; 45 Jeff Kravitz/FilmMagic, Inc/Getty Images; 47 Star Traks/Rex Features; 49 Advertising Archives; 50 Richard Kalvar/Magnum Photos; 51 Benainous-Marouze/Gamma/Getty Images; 53 Rose Hartman/GettyImages; 55 Dave Benett/Getty Images; 56 David/Swindells/PMYCA; 57 Kevin Cummins/Getty Images; 59 Abbas/Magnum Photos; 61 Everett Collection/Rex Features; 63 Richard Young/Rex Features; 65 Getty Images; 67 Paramount/The Kobal Collection; 69 Kevin Cummins/Getty Images; 71 Nick Knight/Trunk Archive; 73 Veville Marriner/Daily Mail/RexFeatures; 74 Richard Young/Rex Features; 75 Mario Testino/Art Partners; 77 Ken Towner/Associated Newspapers/Rex Features; 79 Rex Features; 81 B.D.V/Corbis; 83 Evan Agostini/Getty Images; 85 Chris Moore/Catwalking; 87 Corbis; 89 Thierry Orban/Sygma/Corbis; 91 Richard Young/Rex Features; 93 Retna; 95 Below and Above Kevin Davies; 97 Gareth Watkins/Reuters/Corbis; 99 Rex Features; 101 Anthea Simms; 103 Gary Hershorn/Reuters/Corbis; 105 Bill Cunningham/New York Times/Eyevine; 107 Rex Features.

CREDITS

First published in 2013
by Conran Octopus Ltd
a part of Octopus Publishing
Group, Endeavour House,
189 Shaftesbury Avenue,
London WC2H 8JY
www.octopusbooks.co.uk

An Hachette UK Company
www.hachette.co.uk

Distributed in the US by
Hachette Book Group USA,
237 Park Avenue, New York,
NY 10017 USA

Distributed in Canada by
Canadian Manda Group,
165 Dufferin Street, Toronto,
Ontario, Canada M6K 3H6

British Library Cataloguing-
in-Publication Data.
A catalogue record for this
book is available from the
British Library.

Text written by: Paula Reed

Publisher: Alison Starling
Consultant Editor:
Deyan Sudjic
Senior Editor:
Sybella Stephens
Editor: Robert Anderson
Design: Untitled
Picture Research:
Sara Rumens
Production Controller:
Sarah Kramer

ISBN: 978 1 84091 627 0
Printed in China